Underground

Guided/Group Reading Notes
Lime Band

Contents

OXFORD

Introduction

Reading progression in Year 2/Primary 3

In Year 2/P3 (ages 6–7) children begin to read independently using longer texts containing both familiar words and unfamiliar words that are not completely decodable. The texts at **lime band** continue to include high frequency words. New regular phonetic words including trigraphs and polysyllabic words are used. Topic and subject specific words are introduced in context. Natural sounding language remains the guiding principle.

At lime band children are encouraged to extract meaning from a greater range of genres. The genre and writing styles continue to vary at this level and the text may be presented in a variety of ways. For example, there may be diary entries and letters embedded in the text, flashback might be used or parallel stories told. Dialogue will now be used more extensively to add different layers of understanding about characters' motives and actions.

There are plenty of opportunities within the text for the reader to use inference, deduction and synthesis. A number of 'text only' pages are introduced and illustrations become more incidental. The photographs and illustrations include information that goes well beyond the text to encourage children to draw inferences and so on.

Within the non-fiction texts you will find longer, more formal sentences but still with some repeated terms and structures.

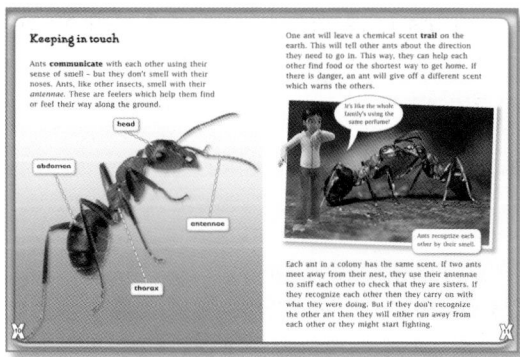

A range of non-fiction features including charts, maps, labelled diagrams, captions, indexes and glossaries are used to encourage children to read and interpret information presented in a variety of ways.

Visual literacy is supported through additional action and information in the illustrations, the use of graphic devices and the suggestions for visualization comprehension strategies suggested in these notes.

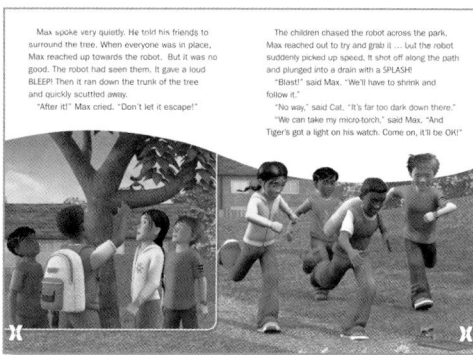

Max spoke very quietly. He told his friends to surround the tree. When everyone was in place, Max reached up towards the robot. But it was no good. The robot had seen them. It gave a loud BLEEP! Then it ran down the trunk of the tree and quickly scuttled away.
"After it!" Max cried. "Don't let it escape!"

The children chased the robot across the park. Max reached out to try and grab it ... but the robot suddenly picked up speed. It shot off along the path and plunged into a drain with a SPLASH!
"Blast!" said Max. "We'll have to shrink and follow it."
"No way," said Cat. "It's far too dark down there."
"We can take my micro-torch," said Max. "And Tiger's got a light on his watch. Come on, it'll be OK!"

Progression in the Project X character books

In this cluster, the central characters continue to develop as they use their amazing micro-watches to have two exciting underground adventures. The overall plot arc is moved on as new characters are introduced, the concept of where the watches come from is explored, as is the idea that someone has been keeping an eye on the children's micro-adventures. In *Ant Meets the Queen*, Max, Cat and Ant explore an ants' nest. Ant's inquisitive nature gets the better of him, but he soon begins to regret it when he is carried away by some worker ants to meet a very hungry looking queen! In *A NASTI Surprise* the children notice that they are being watched by a small green robot, very similar to Ant's pet robot, Rover. They follow the robot into a drain, only to get a nasty shock as it leads them to a strange room – NASTI HQ. In this book, Max feels the burden of leadership as he has to get his friends out of trouble at the end of the story. This is the first book in which we meet the mysterious man in the purple suit (Dr X) and his two henchmen. Links can be made to earlier books by, for example, thinking back to how the children found the watches in *The Silver Box* (Turquoise band, Discovery cluster) and by tracking the introduction and use of Rover and the red robots in *The Thing in the Cupboard* and *Message in an X-bot* (Gold band, Communication cluster).

Guided/group reading

The engaging content and careful levelling of the Project X books makes them ideal for use in guided/group reading sessions. The advantages of using guided/group reading, as well as charts to help you assess the appropriate level for a reading group, are discussed in the *Teaching Handbook* for Year 2/P3.

Speaking, listening and drama

Talk is crucial to learning. Children need plenty of opportunities to express their ideas through talk and drama, and to listen to and watch the ideas of others. These processes are important for building reading engagement, personal response and understanding. Suggestions for speaking, listening, group interaction and drama are given for every book. Within these *Guided/Group Reading Notes* the speaking and listening activities are linked to the reading assessment focuses.

Building comprehension

Understanding what we have read is at the heart of reading. To help readers become effective in comprehending a text these *Guided/Group Reading Notes* contain practical strategies to develop the following important aspects of comprehension:

- Previewing
- Predicting
- Activating and building prior knowledge
- Questioning
- Recalling
- Visualizing and other sensory responses
- Deducing, inferring and drawing conclusions
- Determining importance
- Synthesizing
- Empathizing
- Summarizing
- Personal responses including adopting a critical stance.

The research basis and rationale for focusing on these aspects of comprehension is given in the *Teaching Handbook* for Year 2/P3.

Reading fluency

Reading fluency combines automatic word recognition, reading with pace, and expression. Rereading, fluency and building comprehension are linked together in a complex interrelationship, where each supports the other. This is discussed more fully in the *Teaching Handbook* for Year 2/P3. Opportunities for children to read aloud are important in building fluency and reading aloud to children provides models of expressive fluent reading. Suggestions for purposeful and enjoyable oral reading and rereading/re-listening activities are given in the follow-up activities to guided/group reading and in the notes for parents on the inside cover of each book.

The Project X *Interactive Stories* software can be used to provide a model of reading fluency for the whole class and/or opportunities for individuals or small groups of children to listen to stories again and again. Listening to stories being read is particularly effective with EAL children.

Building vocabulary

Explicit work on enriching vocabulary is important in building reading fluency and comprehension. Repeatedly encountering a word and its variants helps it become known on sight. The thematic 'cluster' structure of Project X supports this because words are repeated within and across the books. Suggestions for vocabulary work are included in these notes. The vocabulary chart on pages 10 and 11 shows when vocabulary is repeated and new words are introduced. It also indicates those words that can be used to support learning alongside a structured phonics and spelling programme.

Developing a thematic approach

Helping children make links in their learning supports their development as learners. All the books in this cluster have a focus on the theme **Underground**. A chart showing the cross-curricular potential of this theme is given in the *Teaching Handbook* for Year 2/P3, along with a rationale for using thematic approaches. Some suggestions for cross-curricular activities are also given in these notes, in the follow-up suggestions for each book.

In guided/group reading sessions, you will also want to encourage children to make links between the books in the cluster. Grouping books in a cluster allows readers to make links between characters, events and actions across the books. This enables readers to gradually build complex understandings of characters, to give reasons why things happen and how characters may change and develop. It can help them recognize cause and effect. It helps children reflect on the skill of determining importance, as a minor incident or detail in one book may prove to have greater significance when considered across several books.

Note that the Project X books in this cluster can be read in any order.

In the **Underground** cluster, some of the suggested links that can be explored across the books include:

- animals and minibeasts that live underground (**Science**)
- the science and geography of rocks and caves (**Science, Geography**)
- Stone Age cave art (**Art and Design**).

Reading into writing

The Project X books provide both models and inspiration to support children's writing. Suggestions for relevant, contextualized and interesting writing activities are given in the follow-up activities for each book. These include both short and longer writing opportunities. The activities cover a wide range of writing contexts so writers can develop an understanding of adapting their writing for different audiences and purposes.

The Project X *Interactive Stories* software contains a collection of 'clip art' assets from the characters books – characters, setting and props – that children can use in their writing.

There are also a number of writing frames that can be downloaded and printed for pupil to use, or that pupils can write/type into directly to practise writing and ICT skills.

Selecting follow-up activities

These *Guided/Group Reading Notes* give many ideas for follow-up activities. Some of these can be completed within the reading session. Some are longer activities that will need to be worked on over time. You should select those activities that are most appropriate for your pupils. It is not expected that you would complete all the suggested activities.

Home/school reading

Books used in a guided/group reading session can also be used in home/school reading programmes.

Before a guided/group reading session, the child could:
- read the first chapter or section of a book
- read a related book from the cluster to build background knowledge.

Following a guided/group reading session, the child could:
- reread the book at home to build reading confidence and fluency
- read the next chapter in a longer book
- read a related book from the cluster.

Advice for parents on supporting their child in reading at home is provided in the inside covers of individual books. There is further advice for teachers concerning home/school reading partnerships in the *Teaching Handbook* for Year 2/P3.

Assessment

During guided/group reading, teachers make ongoing assessments of individuals and of the group. Reading targets are indicated for each book and you should assess against these reading targets. You should select just one or two targets at a time as the focus for the group. The same target can be appropriate for several literacy sessions or over several texts.

Readers should be encouraged to self-assess and peer-assess against the target/s.

Further support for assessing pupils' progress is provided in the *Teaching Handbook* for Year 2/P3.

Continuous reading objectives and ongoing assessment

The following objectives will be supported in *every* guided/group reading session and are therefore a *continuous* focus for attention and assessment. These objectives are not listed in full for each book, but as you listen to individual children reading you should undertake ongoing assessment, against these decoding and encoding objectives:

- Read independently and with increasing fluency longer and less familiar texts **5.1**
- Know how to tackle unfamiliar words that are not completely decodable **5.3**
- Read and spell less common alternative graphemes including trigraphs **5.4**
- Read high and medium frequency words independently and automatically **5.5**

Further objectives are provided as a focus within the notes for each book. Correlation to the specific objectives within the Scottish, Welsh and Northern Ireland curricula are provided in the *Teaching Handbook* for Year 2/P3.

Recording assessment

The assessment chart for the **Underground** cluster is provided on page 51 of the *Teaching Handbook* for Year 2/P3.

Diagnostic assessment

If an individual child is failing to make good progress or he or she seems to have a specific problem with some aspect of reading you will want to undertake a more detailed assessment. Details of how to use running records for diagnostic assessment are given in the *Teaching Handbook* for Year 2/P3.

Vocabulary chart

At Year 2/P3, the children should:

- read high and medium frequency words independently and automatically
- read and spell
  - less common alternative graphemes
  - compound words and polysyllabic words
  - suffixes and prefixes.

A NASTI Surprise	Phonetically regular compound and polysyllabic words	hologram, slowly, whispered, probably, bigger, children, smelly, something, shadows, pictures, everybody, stranded, backpack
	Alternative graphemes including trigraphs	/ay/ (a-e, ai, a) same, place, escape, chased, drain, cables, pale, strange, taken, lady, straight, make, same, waited, safe, later
	Context vocabulary	robot, micro-torch, tunnel, computer screens, control panel, spying, alarm, squeaked, micro-den
Ant Meets the Queen	Phonetically regular compound and polysyllabic words	standing, droppings, football, rabbit, carrot, darkness, several, caterpillar, twenty, himself, hungrily, nearby, thundering, completely, surrounded, rumbling, everything, hopeless, eaten, sadly
	Alternative graphemes including trigraphs	/ee/ (ee, ea, e, y) meets, green, eco, least, knees, peered, three, teased, eat, easily, creeps, these, squeezed, leave, beady, feet, please, been, eaten, he
	Context vocabulary	rabbit, hole, dial, photos, chamber, worker, ants, jaws, passage, larvae, armour, startled, chemical, furry, earthquake, underground

Ants at Home	**Phonetically regular compound and polysyllabic words**	sister, thousands, beneath, colony, survive, insects, shortest, recognize, transparent, temperature, rubbish, compost, summer, exoskeleton
	Alternative graphemes including trigraphs	/igh/ (igh, ie, i, i-e, y) life, like, nightmare, finally, flying, die, survive, direction, find, fighting, might, tidy, outside, I'd, greenflies, sites, sometimes, fight, biting, scientists, dinosaurs
	Context vocabulary	hatches, larva, pupa, adult, wings, hatch, bridge, communicate, feelers, chemical, scent, trail, nursery, temperature, farmer, fungus, honeydew, soldier, stomach
The Knockits of Knockity Hoo	**Phonetically regular compound and polysyllabic words**	weekend, information grinning, speaking, drumming, sunshine, summer, everything, surprise, excitement, adventure, fantastic
	Alternative graphemes including trigraphs	/ow/ (ow, o, o-e, oe) no, phone, hole, home, folk, mobile, photo, low, nowhere, stony, follow, go, open, nosy, holes, don't, know, told, joked, following, old, tiptoes, homes, only, hello
	Context vocabulary	Knockity Hoo, mobile phone, ring tone, Overground, finders keepers, nooks, stony, darkness, follow-my-leader, rhythms, party-pushers, Midsummer Whoopee, drummer
Going Underground	**Phonetically regular compound and polysyllabic words**	underground, different, animals, morning, grasshoppers, lizards, scorpions, bedtime, goodnight, seabirds, outside, pot-hole, stretcher, prehistoric, electricity
	Alternative graphemes including trigraphs	/oo/ (oo, ou, o) food, cool, to, you, do, group, cocoon, two, onto, soon, rooms, cool, room, schools, who
	Context vocabulary	meerkats, burrow, miner, grasshoppers, grubs, abdomen, cocoons, antennae, puffin, mountain, mammals, echo, passages, shaft, stretcher, Lascaux, Metro, Dinorwig, power station, Matmata, Tunisia, Sahara Desert

A NASTI Surprise

BY TONY BRADMAN

	Literacy Framework objective	Target and assessment focus
Speaking, listening, group interaction and drama	○ Explain their reactions to texts, commenting on important aspects **8.3**	○ We can tell others about our favourite part of the story **AF3**
Reading See also continuous reading objectives listed on page 9.	○ Draw together ideas and information from across a whole text **7.1** ○ Give some reasons why things happen or characters change **7.2**	○ We can explain the main events of the story in a clear sequence **AF4** ○ We can say why characters do some of the things that they do **AF3**

The following notes provide a structure for up to two guided/group reading sessions. They are intended to be used flexibly; you may choose to focus on both sessions or you could focus on one session and have the children read the rest of the book independently.

In Session 1, children will read Chapters 2 and 3 after you read Chapter 1 to them. In Session 2 children will read to the end of the book.

Session 1 (Chapters 1–3)

Before reading

To activate prior knowledge and encourage prediction

- Ask whether any of the children have ever looked inside a drain. (Maybe something got lost down one?) Discuss what they could hear, feel, smell and see. If no one has ever looked down a drain, show pictures and describe what drains are like e.g. cold, damp, dark, smelly.

- Look at the cover and pose the question: What does NASTI stand for? You will need to draw out the distinction from 'nasty'. Ask children to discuss in pairs. This could be extended by getting one pair to share ideas with another pair, depending on the size of the group (*think, pair, share*). Review what is already known about the characters.

To support decoding and word recognition and introduce new vocabulary

- Check understanding of key vocabulary: scuttled (p.6), picked up speed (p.7), plunged (p.7), micro-size (p.8). If necessary, help children to decode the words. Discuss the words' meanings and why these words and phrases have been used. Add these to a class collection of descriptive language (verbs as well as adjectives), either on a word wall or in a class word book. This can be added to as children read other stories in this cluster.

To engage readers and support fluent reading

- Read the first chapter to the children, modelling fluency and use of voice to make the story interesting.

During reading

- Remind the children what to do if they encounter a difficult word: use phonic skills first; look for parts of the word they know; read on or back to get the context of the sentence; use any picture clues.

- Ask the children to read the next chapter independently. Then invite them to predict what will happen next: what will the characters do, what will the green robot do? This could be differentiated by giving sentence starters, e.g. The children can see... ; The green robot has... ; The children will follow the robot because... (**predicting**)

- Then ask the children to read the next chapter of the book. You could also try getting them to read as pairs, or periodically read round the group.

- As they read, ask the children to think about what the characters did (followed a strange robot into a dangerous place) and why they might have done this. Was it sensible? The children could also consider why the green robot ran away. (**deducing**, **inferring**)

· ·>

Assessment point

Listen to individual children reading and make ongoing assessments on their decoding/sight vocabulary approaches to tackling new words and their reading fluency AF1

After reading

Returning to the text

- Ask the children to predict how the story could end. This could be recorded in note form as a group and then compared to the actual ending. (**predicting**)

- Ask children whether they think the green robot was leading the characters down into the drain and if so why that might be. What did it want? Sentence starters may help less confident pupils, e.g. I think he led them into the drain because...; I think it wanted... because... (**drawing conclusions, inferring**)

Building comprehension

- Based on what each character has done and said so far, can the children start to build up a profile on each one? e.g. Cat doesn't like the dark (p.7) and hates bad smells (p.10); Max seems to be the leader ('I'll go first' on p.10). This could be recorded on the *Character grid* Photocopy Master.

> **Assessment point**
>
> Can children share ideas and make reference to the text itself to justify their ideas about the characters? AF3

Session 2 (Chapters 4–5)

Before reading

To activate prior knowledge and encourage prediction

- Recap the story and review the children's predictions from Session 1.

During reading

- Ask the children to read from chapter 4 to the end of the book.

- As you listen to individual children read, you might want to ask them to stop and summarize what has happened so far and predict what will happen next. (**summarizing, predicting**)
- Alternatively, you may want the whole group to stop after page 27 and recap what has happened so far. (**summarizing**)

After reading

Returning to the text
- Discuss whether the children's predictions were right.
- Use pictures from key points of the story. Give some of these out, with some key points missing. Challenge the children to say which ones might be missing, write missing bits on card and then order them (cards and pictures) correctly.

- >

Assessment point
Can children explain the main events of the story? Can they offer reasons for the order they describe? **AF4**

- Ask the children which character they liked least and their reasons for their choice. (**personal response**)
- Invite children to choose their favourite moment in the story and explain why. (**personal response**)

- >

Assessment point
Can children tell others about their favourite part of the story? Can they listen to the ideas of other pupils and can they say if they agree or disagree with what has been said? **AF3**

Follow-up activities

Writing activities
- Write a retelling of the story with a different ending. (**longer writing task**)
- Add to/start the *Character grids* Photocopy Master for Ant, Max and the others. Compare what the characters are like and use this to write a short passage in support of their choice of favourite character. (**short writing task**)

Other literacy activities

- Children could retell the story from the green robot's point of view, using the pictures from the ordering activity in Session 2. It would also be useful to do the 'hot seating' activity to unpick thoughts and feeling of the robot (see *Ask the robot!* Photocopy Master).

- Design a wanted poster that the man in the underground den might have printed for one of the characters (Ant, Cat, etc).

- Use the sequencing pictures to play 'I Spy'. (Probably best to use one or two pictures at a time, unless you are very good at guessing!)

Cross-curricular and thematic opportunities

- Design a 'spy' robot to get secret information about: what parents have got you for your birthday etc. (**DT**)

- Use the information in the book (mostly via pictures) to support Internet research about what is under the ground, e.g. drains, telephone cables, gas pipes. (**ICT, Geography**)

- Discuss the children's decision to follow the robot down the drain. Talk about whether this was a sensible/ safe action. Draw out discussion about things that seem exciting but that are not safe to do and why. Talk about how things are different in fiction books from in real life. (**PSHE**)

Ant Meets the Queen

BY JAN BURCHETT AND SARA VOGLER

About this book

When Max, Cat and Ant go down a rabbit hole they discover a colony of ants. And Ant gets more than he bargained for!

You will need

- Pictures of digging tools (or toy versions)
- *Character clues* Photocopy Master 72, *Teaching Handbook* for Year 2/P3
- *Tunnel game* Photocopy Master 73, *Teaching Handbook* for Year 2/P3

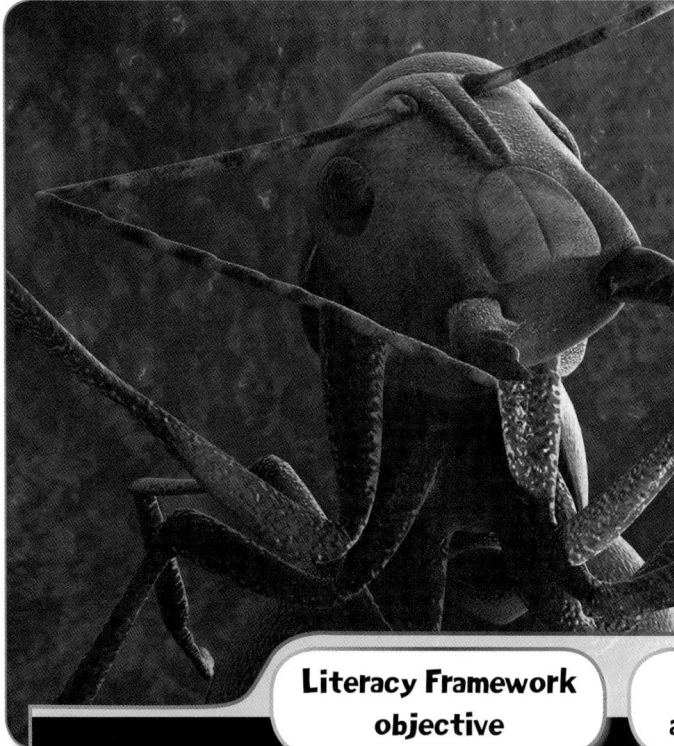

	Literacy Framework objective	Target and assessment focus
Speaking, listening, group interaction and drama	○ Explain their reactions to texts, commenting on important aspects **8.3**	○ We can tell others about our favourite character **AF3**
Reading See also continuous reading objectives listed on page 9.	○ Draw together ideas and information from across a whole text **7.1** ○ Give some reasons why things happen or characters change **7.2**	○ We can explain the main events of the story in a clear sequence **AF4** ○ We can say how characters are feeling and why **AF3**

The following notes provide a structure for up to two guided/group reading sessions. They are intended to be used flexibly; you may choose to focus on both sessions or you could focus on one session and have the children read the rest of the book independently.

In Session 1, children will read Chapter 2 after you read Chapter 1 to them. In Session 2 children will read to the end of the book.

Session 1 (Chapters 1–2)

Before reading

To activate prior knowledge and encourage prediction

- Ask whether any of the children have ever done any digging. If they have, discuss how it felt e.g. hot, lots of pushing, hurt their hands, dirty. If no one has had this experience then talk about what it feels like and show some pictures of digging tools or handle some toy tools.

- Look at the cover and pose the question: Do you think it means Queen Elizabeth II? Invite children to discuss in pairs. This could be extended by getting one pair to share ideas with another pair, depending on the size of the group (*think, pair, share*).

To support decoding and word recognition and introduce new vocabulary

- Check understanding of key vocabulary: eco (p.2), tunnel (p.3), chamber (p.10). If necessary, help children to decode the words. Discuss their meaning and why these words are better than alternatives like: new, pathway, room. Start or continue a collection of descriptive language (verbs as well as adjectives), either on a word wall or in a class word book. This can be added to as children read other stories in this cluster.

To engage readers and support fluent reading

- Read the first chapter to the children, modelling fluency and use of voice to make the story interesting. At the end of the chapter, ask them to predict what will happen next, e.g. What do the children see? What will they do next? This could be differentiated by giving sentence starters, e.g. Through gap the children can see... ; The children will go on because/go back because...

During reading

- Ask the children to read the next chapter of the book independently. You could also try getting them to read as pairs, or periodically read round the group.

- Remind the children about what to do if they encounter a difficult word: use phonic skills first; look for parts of the word they know; read on or back to get the context of the sentence; use any picture clues.

- As they read, ask the children to think about what the children did (went on an adventure without Tiger) and why they might have done this.

- Invite the children to predict how the story could end. This could be recorded in note form as a group and then compared to the actual ending. (**predicting**)

Assessment point
Listen to individual children reading and make ongoing assessments on their decoding/sight vocabulary approaches to tackling new words and their reading fluency AF1

After reading

Returning to the text

- Ask children why they think Tiger was left out of this adventure. (**inferring**)
- Discuss how Max, Cat and Ant are feeling at the point when Ant is taken away and why they feel the way they do. (**empathizing**)

· ·>

Building Comprehension

- Ask the children whether they themelves would have followed Ant through the hole into the ant nest and what would it have felt like to be carried off by the ants. Can they explain their ideas?

Session 2 (Chapters 3–5)

Before reading

To activate prior knowledge and encourage prediction

- Recap the story and review the children's predictions from Session 1.

During reading

- Ask the children to read from Chapter 3 to the end of the book.
- As you listen to individual children read, you might want to ask them to stop and summarize what has happened so far and predict what will happen next. (**summarizing, predicting**)
- Alternatively, you may want the whole group to stop after page 24 and recap what has happened so far. (**summarizing**)

After reading

Returning to the text

- Ask children to sequence the story by drawing pictures of the key points from memory. Together, discuss any differences between the children's sequences, and then check with the book. (**summarizing**)

....>

- Ask the children which character they liked best and their reasons for their choice.

....>

- Play a game with the *Character clues* Photocopy Master. In groups of four, children cut up the character clues and place them face down. In pairs they select a clue, discuss it, and then decide which character it belongs to. As the game progresses the children should be building up character profiles. When the cards are all selected, the pairs team up and swap clues so that they have complete profiles. (NB: some characters have more clues than others and some clues could belong with more than one character.)

Building comprehension

- Ask the children why Max wanted Ant to take a photo. (**inferring**) (To startle the ant queen with the flash - she is not used to light like that as she only lives underground in the dark.)

Building fluency

- Play 'pass the story'. One pupil starts to retell the story and then passes it on to the next child... and so on round the group. The teacher may need to fill in any gaps.

Follow-up activities

Writing activities

- Children could write an alternative ending for the story from where Ant gets carried off. (**longer writing task**)
- Ask children to pretend to be Tiger. They have to design a missing poster for his friends, with a short description of them and where they were last seen. (**short writing task**)

Other literacy activities

- Children could retell the story as a group, with each person taking on a character. This could be performed for the rest of the class. Digital photos of this could be used in a simple text, created using presentation software.
- Children could make cut-outs of the characters and use these to act out the story, like a short play. (**drama**)
- Select small sections of text from the story and a matching picture and stick them onto card (a maximum of four sections to make eight cards). Place the cards face down and turn over one at a time. Children have to try and remember where the pairs are.

Cross-curricular and thematic opportunities

- Play the *Tunnel game* Photocopy Master. This is like snakes and ladders and will enable children to practise playing with dice and counting on. (**Maths**)
- Design an 'ant facts' poster showing interesting facts about ants, using information in the book and from Internet and book research. (**Science, ICT**)
- Challenge the children to design and build an 'underground' home suitable for a colony of ants, with tunnels and other features. (**DT**)
- Can the children find out about any other creatures that have a queen? (e.g. bees) (**Science**)
- Engage the children in gardening activities in a school garden or in the classroom. (**Science**)

Ants at Home

BY HAYDN MIDDLETON

About this book

Max and Cat shrink and go underground to explore the world of ants.

You will need

- *Ant facts* Photocopy Master 74, *Teaching Handbook* for Year 2/P3

	Literacy Framework objective	Target and assessment focus
Speaking, listening, group interaction and drama	○ Explain their reactions to texts, commenting on important aspects **8.3**	○ We can explain our ideas to others and refer to the text **AF3**
Reading See also continuous reading objectives listed on page 9.	○ Draw together ideas and information from across a whole text, using simple signposts in the text **7.1** ○ Explain organizational features of texts, including diagrams ... **7.3**	○ We can recall key information/facts from a text and give reasons for our opinions **AF2/4**

The following notes provide a structure for up to two guided/group reading sessions. They are intended to be used flexibly; you may choose to focus on both sessions or you could focus on one session and have the children read the rest of the book independently.

In Session 1, children will read pages 8–13 after you read pages 2–7 to them. In Session 2 children will read to the end of the book.

Session 1 (Pages 2–13)

? Before reading

To activate prior knowledge and encourage prediction

- Ask whether the children have ever watched ants in the garden, or seen inside their nest. Discuss what it might look and feel like. Ask them to draw what an ant home might look like. (**predicting**)

- Using the *Ant facts* Photcopy Master, list quite quickly what is already known about ants.

- Look at the cover and pose the question: What would you like to find out about ants from this book? Invite children to discuss in pairs. This could be extended by getting one pair to share ideas with another pair, depending on the size of the group (*think*, *pair*, *share*). List some of the suggestions and then see if the contents page shows this information.

To support decoding and word recognition and introduce new vocabulary

- Check understanding of key vocabulary: raft (p.9), temperature (p.13), milking (p.19), crops (p.18), fungus (p.18), transparent (p.12). If necessary, help children to decode the words. Discuss their meaning and link this to the glossary in the book. Start or continue a collection of descriptive language (verbs as well as adjectives and nouns), either on a word wall or in a class word book.

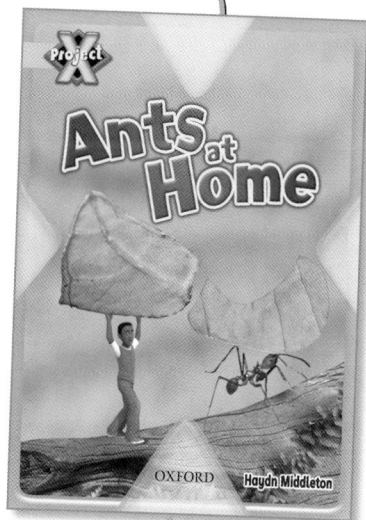

This can be added to as children read other books in this cluster.

To engage readers and support fluent reading

- Read pages 2–7 to the children, modelling fluency and use of voice to make the information interesting. At the end of the section ask them to predict how the ant home might be different from the picture they drew earlier. This could be differentiated by giving sentence starters e.g. The ants are... so they will need/won't need...; Ant homes will be small because....

During reading

- Remind the children about what to do if they encounter a difficult word: use phonic skills first; look for parts of the word they know; read on or back to get the context of the sentence; use any picture clues.
- Ask the children to read independently pages 8–13. You could also try getting them to read as pairs, or periodically read round the group.
- You could also ask them to find one thing about ants that they really like and share this with the group after reading the text.

> **Assessment point**
>
> Listen to individual children reading and make ongoing assessments on their decoding/sight vocabulary approaches to tackling new words and their reading fluency AF1

··>

After reading

Returning to the text

- Use pictures from key information points in the text. Ask differentiated questions about these pages, e.g. Which ant lays all the eggs? (p.6); Why do you think only the queen lays eggs? (p.6); How did the ants get across a gap? (p.9)

> **Assessment point**
>
> Listen to answers given. Note those who are able to offer answers and whether they make reference to the text itself to justify their opinion. AF2/4

··>

- Ask children in pairs to compare their picture of an ant home to the picture on page 8. Ask the children to say which bits they got right and which bits they had not thought about. Decide which person came up with most of the aspects of an ant home in their own drawing, e.g. room for babies, tunnels to join rooms and get outside, underground, small.

· >

- Invite the children to share their favourite fact about ants with the rest of the group.

Building Comprehension

- Ask the children how ants communicate (smell) and whether this is better than talking. This is in the text on pages 10 and 11. Sentence starters could be used e.g. It would be no use ants talking because...; Talking would be better because... (**deducing, inferring**)

Session 2 (Pages 14–24)

Before reading

To activate prior knowledge and encourage prediction

- Use the *Ant facts* Photocopy Master from Session 1 to recap what the children knew about ants before they started reading. Review what they learned in Session 1 by adding in new information to column two.

During reading

- As they read, ask the children to think about which job they would like/not like to do in an ant colony and say why they think this. (**personal response**)

- If you have not already done so, ask the children what to do if they encounter a difficult word, modelling with an example from the book if necessary. Praise children who successfully decode unfamiliar words.

After reading

Returning to the text

- Return to a discussion of ant jobs, encouraging children to explain their preferences, showing an understanding of the organization of the text.
- Together, recall the foods that ants like to eat.

· ·→

> **Assessment point**
>
> Can the children recall information from the text? AF2/4

Building fluency

- Play 'One ant went to chew, went to chew a leaf up' to the tune of 'One man went to mow'. The children need to list either things ants have or what they do, e.g. One ant and his antennae went to chew a leaf up, two ants went... (**recall**)

Follow-up activities

Writing activities

- Children could discuss how the layout, photographs and diagrams have been used in the book and then use a template from simple presentation software to build up an interactive non-fiction text about ants/insects/creepy crawlies. (**longer writing task**)
- Children could create and design a menu that would appeal to an ant. They could do this on paper or using a suitable computer program. (**short writing task**)

Other literacy activities

- Play 'I'm thinking of a creature'. Give simple clues, e.g. I'm thinking of a creature that has six legs... (child guesses ant). No, this creature always has wings – child guesses correctly 'fly'.

- Play a quick word game in pairs. Challenge the children to write down as many words as they can that feature 'ant', e.g. important, mantle, elephant.

Cross-curricular and thematic opportunities

- Children could design a uniform for the soldier ants, relating to the sort of protection needed if poison is spit at them, or they are bitten, as well as general things like boots to protect feet from hard ground. (**DT**)

- Use the information in the book (mostly via pictures) to support Internet research about ants and other insects. This could be included in the interactive book from the longer writing task. (**ICT, Science**)

- In a Circle Time session discuss how ants all work together in a colony. Draw out ideas about how the children can work well with one another. (**PSHE**)

Making a home

Ant nests are full of underground tunnels. Sometimes two teams of ants will work together to make a tunnel. Each team starts digging at a different end. Ants are very good planners and know exactly where to meet in the middle.

This bridge is really strong!

It's dark in these tunnels!

These ants are making a bridge together.

To get across a gap, ants will plan and build a bridge – out of themselves!

Some ants build water traps in their nest in the earth. If it rains hard, these traps catch the water and stop any flooding. To survive floods, ants team up to become a floating **raft**.

The Knockits of Knockity Hoo

BY MAUREEN HASELHURST

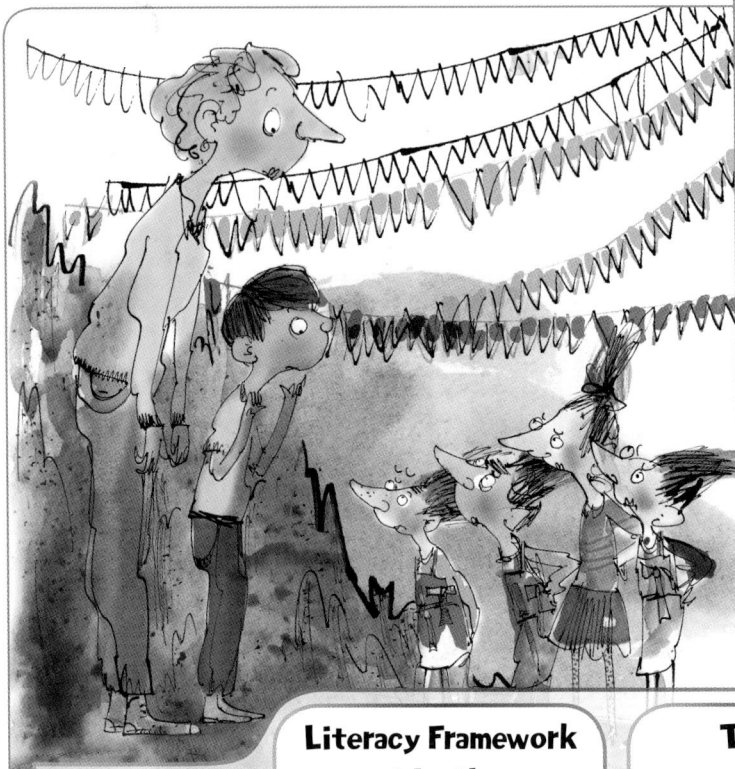

About this book

A family venture into the caves of Knockity Hoo and discover the strange people called the Knockits that live there.

You will need

- Pictures of caves (inside and out)
- *Digby* Photocopy Master 75, *Teaching Handbook* for Year 2/P3
- *Character chart* Photocopy Master 76, *Teaching Handbook* for Year 2/P3

	Literacy Framework objective	Target and assessment focus
Speaking, listening, group interaction and drama	○ Engage with books through exploring and enacting interpretations **8.2**	○ We can say how we think the story will end **AF3**
Reading See also continuous reading objectives listed on page 9.	○ Give some reasons why things happen or characters change **7.2**	○ We can say why characters do some of the things that they do **AF3**

The following notes provide a structure for up to two guided/group reading sessions. They are intended to be used flexibly; you may choose to focus on both sessions or you could focus on one session and have the children read the rest of the book independently.

In Session 1, children will read Chapter 2 after you read Chapter 1 to them. In Session 2 children will read to the end of the book.

Session 1 (Chapters 1–2)

Before reading

To activate prior knowledge and encourage prediction

- Ask whether any of the children have ever been in a cave. Discuss what they could hear, feel, smell and see. If no one has had this experience then show pictures and describe what caves are like, e.g. cold, damp, dark.

- Have a go at 'echoing'. The teacher says a word and the children repeat it as an echo, one after the other. Try to get quieter with each repetition.

- Look at the cover and pose the question: Why might these people be called Knockits? Invite children to discuss in pairs. This could be extended by asking one pair to share ideas with another pair, depending on the size of the group. (**predicting**)

To support decoding and word recognition and introduce new vocabulary

- Check understanding of key vocabulary such as: trilled (p.7), scrambled (p.13), flickering (p.13), maze (p.14). If necessary, help children to decode the words. Discuss their meaning and why these words are better than alternatives like: rang, walked, lighted, many. Start or continue a collection of descriptive language (verbs as well as adjectives), either on a word wall or in a class word book.

To engage readers and support fluent reading
- Read the first chapter to the children, modelling fluency and use of voice to make the story interesting.

During reading

- Ask the children to read the next chapter independently. You could also try getting them to read as pairs, or periodically read round the group.
- Ask the children what to do if they encounter a difficult word, modelling with an example from the book if necessary. Praise children who successfully decode unfamiliar words.

> **Assessment point**
>
> Listen to individual children reading and make ongoing assessments on their decoding, sight vocabulary, approaches to tackling new words and their reading fluency. **AF1**

- As they read, ask the children to think about what the Knockit did (taking the mobile phone) and why he might have done this. They could also consider whether the 'Overgrounders' did the right thing in following Digby, or be asked to explain what is meant by 'finders keepers'. (**inferring, adopting a critical stance**)

After reading

Returning to the text
- Ask children why they think Digby wanted the 'Overgrounders' to follow him underground. (**deducing, inferring**)
- Ask the children which character they like best so far and their reasons for their choice. (**personal response**)

Building comprehension
- Ask the children to predict how the story could end. This could be recorded in note form as a group and then compared to the actual ending. (**predicting**)

> **Assessment point**
>
> Can children predict how the story will end? **AF3**

Session 2 (Chapters 3–5)

Before reading

To activate prior knowledge and encourage prediction

- Recap what has happened in the story so far. Review the notes from Session 1 in which the children made predictions about the ending of the story. Discuss what the children think will happen next; what will the children do, what will the adults do, what will the Knockits do? This could be differentiated by giving sentence starters e.g. The Knockits will invite the people to join the party because... or The Knockits will run away and hide because... (**predicting**)

During reading

- Ask the children to read from Chapter 3 to the end of the book.
- As you listen to individual children read, you might want to ask them to stop and summarize what has happened so far and predict what will happen next. (**summarizing, predicting**)
- Alternatively, you may want the whole group to stop after page 29 and recap what has happened so far. (**summarizing**)

After reading

- Use pictures from key points of the story. Put these out in the wrong order and ask the children if it is correct. Challenge them to say what the order should be and why they think this. (**recalling**)

Building comprehension

- Ask the children how Digby was different from the other Knockits, e.g. not being angry with the 'overgrounders' for: crashing the party, digging holes. This is in the text on pages 18–19 and 24–25. Follow this up with what they think Digby would enjoy most in the 'Overground'. Remind them of his love for music. Use the *Digby* Photocopy Master to explore children's understanding of the character. (**synthesizing**)

· ·>

Assessment point
Can children say why characters do some of the things that they do? **AF3**

- Use the *Character chart* Photocopy Master to explore the other characters in the book. It provides a framework to prompt children to assess characters' personalities by giving reasons from the text as evidence.

Building fluency

- Play 'pass the story'. One child starts to retell the story and then passes it on to the next child… and so on round the group. The teacher may need to fill in any gaps.

Follow-up activities

Writing activities

- Children could write an invitation to the Knockits' Whoopee. (**short writing task**)
- Children could write a retelling of the story to put into a class collection of stories they have enjoyed. (**longer writing task**)

Other literacy activities

- Children could retell the story as a group, with each person taking on a character. This could be performed for the rest of the class. (**drama**)
- Play 'Follow my leader' with hand claps. The teacher

models and the children mirror the claps. This will help develop listening skills. (**listening**)

- Stick small sections of the story text and a matching picture onto card (maximum of four sections to make eight cards). Place the sentences and pictures face down and turn over one at a time. The child has to remember where the pairs are. The same cards could be used for snap.

Cross-curricular and thematic opportunities

- Design a poster advertising the Knockits' Whoopee. (**Art and design**)
- Children could make cut-outs of the characters and use these to act out the story, like a short play. This is especially good if they are less confident in performing. Digital photos of this could be used in a simple presentation. (**Drama, ICT**)
- Use the book's pictures to support Internet research about caves in your locality. (**ICT, Geography**)
- Challenge the children to create their own percussion instruments using junk materials like cardboard boxes and empty containers. Can they create a group performance? (**Music, DT**)

Going Underground

BY JOHN MALAM

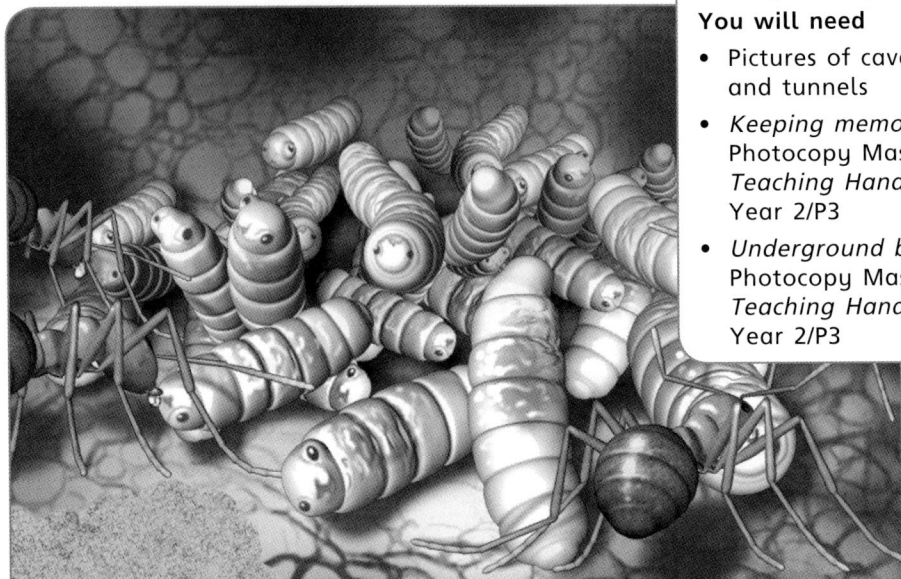

About this book

This non-fiction book is all about animals that live underground. It also shows some human activity underground.

You will need

- Pictures of caves and tunnels
- *Keeping memories* Photocopy Master 77, *Teaching Handbook* for Year 2/P3
- *Underground bingo* Photocopy Master 78, *Teaching Handbook* for Year 2/P3

	Literacy Framework objective	**Target and assessment focus**
Speaking, listening, group interaction and drama	○ Work effectively in groups by ensuring that each group member takes a turn challenging, supporting and moving on **3.2**	○ We can work together as a group and listen to each other's ideas **AF2**
Reading See also continuous reading objectives listed on page 9.	○ Draw together ideas and information from across a whole text **7.1** ○ Explain organizational features of texts, including layout, diagrams, captions **7.3**	○ We can recall and retrieve key information from a text **AF2** ○ We can recognise organizational features of a non-fiction text **AF4**

The following notes provide a structure for up to two guided/group reading sessions. They are intended to be used flexibly; you may choose to focus on both sessions or you could focus on one session and have the children read the rest of the book independently.

In Session 1, children will read pages 8–15 after you read pages 2–7 to them. In Session 2 children will read to the end of the book.

Session 1 (Pages 2–15)

Before reading

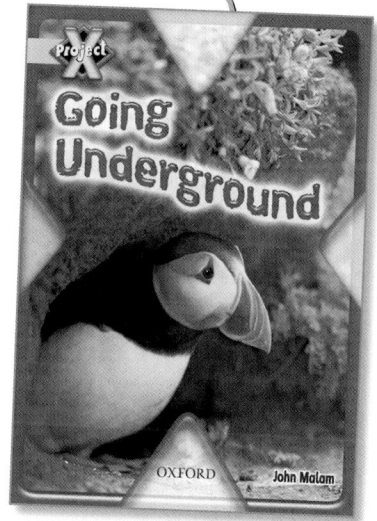

To activate prior knowledge and encourage prediction

- Ask whether the children have ever been underground (in a cave or through the channel tunnel). Discuss what it looks, feels and smells like. If no one has had this experience then show pictures.

- Look at the cover and pose the question: What do you think we will find out about from this book? List some of the suggestions and then compare to the contents page. (**predicting**)

To support decoding and word recognition and introduce new vocabulary

- Check understanding of key prepositional vocabulary: under/ underground, outside/out of, into/in/inside, on/onto/at the end of. If necessary, support children in decoding the words. Discuss and model their practical meaning.

To engage readers and support fluent reading

- Read pages 2–7 to the children, modelling fluency and use of voice to make the information interesting. Support the children in noticing and reading non-fiction features such as labels and captions.

During reading

- Ask the children to read the next three sections (as far as page 15) independently.

- Remind the children about what to do if they encounter a difficult word: use phonic skills first; look for parts of the word they know; read on or back to get the context of the sentence; use any picture clues.

Assessment point

Listen to individual children reading and make ongoing assessments on their decoding/sight vocabulary approaches to tackling new words and their reading fluency **AF1**

· ·>

- As they read ask the children to think about which animal they like the best and why.

- You could also ask them to find one thing that really interested them about the 'underground', either fascinating facts or cute animals. These could be recorded in note form and returned to later for a writing activity. (**personal response**)

After reading

Returning to the text

- Ask children to respond to either the question about which animal they liked best, or interesting things they found out.

- Discuss how the writer has organized the information to make it interesting and easy to read (organizational features). Together, create a list of features such as: pictures, captions, labels, bullet points.

Assessment point

Can the children recognize organizational features of non-fiction texts? Can they recall and retrieve information from the text? **AF2/AF4**

· ·>

Building Comprehension

- Use pictures from key information points in the text. Ask differentiated questions about these pages, e.g. What do puffins feed their young?; If a puffin has six fish already, how many more could it hold in its beak? (p.13) Where do bats sleep?; Why do bats sleep upside down? (p.15)

Session 2 (Pages 16–23)

⟨?⟩ Before reading

To activate prior knowledge and encourage prediction
- Recap the information that was learned from reading up to page 15. Children could refer to their notes of interesting facts and favourite animals from Session 1.

📖 During reading

- Ask the children to read from page 16 to the end of the book.
- As you listen to individual children read, you might want to ask them to stop and summarize what they have learned so far. (**summarizing**)

🔍 After reading

- Ask children to focus on page 22 'City of the future?'. Challenge them to think about what might be better/worse about living underground, e.g. If you lived underground how would playing out be different/the same/better?; What do you think schools would be like? Encourage them to comment on each others' views.

> **Assessment point**
>
> Can children work together as a group and listen to each others' ideas? AF2

∙∙∙∙∙∙∙∙∙∙∙∙∙∙∙∙∙∙∙∙∙∙∙∙∙∙∙∙∙∙∙∙∙∙∙∙∙∙∙➤

Building Comprehension
- Ask the children how we keep a memory of a special thing or event now (video camera, photographs, scrap book, diary). Ask how this is the same and different from the way that prehistoric people kept memories at Lascaux (pp.18–19). Use the *Keeping memories* Photocopy Master to make comparisons in a written table.

- Return to page 20 and ask children to write on sticky notes reasons why the power station needed to be hidden. Also, come up with reasons why it should be built in the countryside, e.g. it costs too much to hide it.

Building fluency

- Invite children to reread pages 16–17 'Cave rescue'. Encourage them to act out the scene, putting all the events into the right order. Alternatively, cards with events on could be ordered into the correct sequence.

Follow-up activities

Writing activities

- Children could write a menu that would appeal to a meerkat. (**short writing task**)
- Use the information in the book and Internet research to write a class book about the world underground. (**longer writing task**)

Other literacy activities

- Children could use the information written on sticky notes in Session 2 to take part in a 'conscience alley'. The children make a corridor with children on each side and the teacher walks between the two lines. The teacher takes a step and gives a reason why the power station should not be hidden. The children can then counter with an idea from the sticky notes.
- Play *Underground bingo* using the Photocopy Master. This game is based on prepositions.

Cross-curricular and thematic opportunities

- Using pages 18–19 as a stimulus and some Internet research on cave paintings, invite the children to create their own paintings in a similar style. (**Art, ICT**)
- Challenge the children to design their own underground dens of the future. Support this task by discussing all the things that the children might want and need in their den. (**Art and design**)